Let's go travel

Travel Journal

Belongs to:

_____

_____

_____

_____

Date: _____

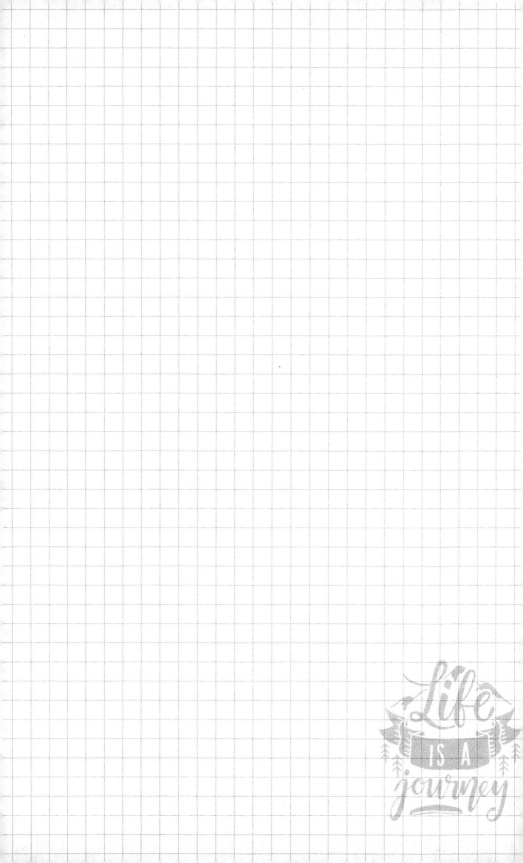

ADDRESSES AND
NOTES

TO DO:

TO DO:

HOTELS-CAMPS-ACCOMODATIONS

-
-
-
-
-
-
-
-
-
-
-

HOTELS-CAMPS-ACCOMODATIONS:

HOTELS-CAMPS-ACCOMODATIONS

-
-
-
-
-
-
-
-
-
-
-

RESTAURANTS etc.

RESTAURANTS etc.

-
-
-
-
-
-
-
-
-
-
-

RESTAURANTS etc.

SHOPPING

SHOPPING

SHOPPING

BARS etc:

BARS etc:

-
-
-
-
-
-
-
-
-
-
-

ADDRESSES:

ADDRESSES:

ADDRESSES:

ADDRESSES:

NEW CONTACTS:

NEW CONTACTS:

NEW CONTACTS:

NEW CONTACTS:

Made in the USA
Monee, IL
14 November 2021